THE BEST OF

1995

'Typical ! You wait 25 years
for a ceasefire and then
suddenly two come along'

MATTHEW PRITCHETT
was voted Granada's
What the Papers Say
Cartoonist of the Year
in 1992. He studied at
St Martin's School of
Art in London and first
saw himself published in
the *New Statesman* during
one of its rare lapses from
high seriousness. He has
been *The Daily Telegraph*'s
front-page pocket
cartoonist since 1988.

The Daily Telegraph

THE BEST OF

1995

'*At least we know you're
not taking performance-
enhancing drugs*'

ORION

Orion Books
A Division of the Orion Publishing Group Ltd
Orion House
5 Upper St Martin's Lane
London WC2H 9EA

Second impression 1996

First published by Orion Books 1995

The right of Matthew Pritchett to be identified as the
author of this work has been asserted by him in accordance
with the Copyright, Designs and Patents Act, 1988

A CIP catalogue record for this book is available
from the British Library

ISBN 1 75280 292 5

Printed and bound in Great Britain by
The Guernsey Press Co. Ltd, Guernsey, Channel Islands

THE BEST OF

Politics

'No, not victory–that's how many votes I got'

'We'll meet again, don't know where...'

Tories stumble at local elections...

Politics

'My hiccups completely vanished after that man said he intended to vote Conservative at the next election'

'I was going to vote Tory but I made a last minute shambolic U-turn'

Politics

'This is Lord Lucan. I think
I've spotted a Tory voter'

Politics

'This used to be a
hospital, Mrs Bottomley'

Major wobbles and changes his Cabinet

Politics

'I nearly saw
something then'

'It's Tony Blair rock – it says
nothing all the way through'

New Labour show its colours

Politics

'I've named this one after Sir Jerry Wiggin – it's called Sebastian Coe'

'Mr and Mrs Sebastian Coe'

Sir Jerry Wiggin reveals a hidden identity, but not his interests ...

Politics

'It's not my fault — God gave me sleaze genes'

'I don't remember signing this'

Politics

After the payment for questions scandal comes
the forced declaration of business interests

Politics

'I feel I'm a Labour
candidate trapped inside
a man's body'

'I'm not making up my mind
until we've had the
swimwear section'

Labour ward – women only

Politics

'I suppose Prime Ministers
must get some weird thrill
from the risks of a
leadership election'

MEMBERS' DINING
ROOM

'Two ordered the steak but
really want the fish, three
couldn't decide, and the rest
are waiting for the next course'

The P.M. announces his step
down as Tory leader as film star
Hugh Grant is caught with his
pants down

And the backbenches look to a
number of potential candidates
for Tory leader

Politics

'It's loyalty, PM, but
not as we know it'

'Past Redwood's HQ, left at
Major's HQ, left again at
Portillo's HQ and it's
opposite Heseltine's HQ'

First stalking horse, John Redwood, is likened to
a Vulcan (no human emotions) but he's not the
only candidate

Politics

'If I connect the
yellow and blue wires
Teresa Gorman is PM'

'Quick everyone
back onboard'

But in the end the party unites
behind Major

Politics

'Well, Sir Richard, just hold
your Scott Report under water
and you'll see bubbles coming
from where the leak is'

'I think I've forgotten
what the Scott inquiry
was supposed to be about'

Arms to Iraq inquiry goes on and on under the
cycling judge Scott

Northern Ireland peace initiative

'We want you to defuse
Ian Paisley'

'It's a complete conservatory,
but I'm not saying
it's permanent'

The framework for peace is a very carefully
worded document

Fishing dispute

'You should see the one
that didn't get away'

'Just a minute! This breaches
EC fishing regulations'

Undersized fish

Fishing dispute

'Oh no, I've got a
Spanish fish finger'

'If I can just catch a fish a
Canadian boat is bound
to show up'

The Canadians send warships
to intercept the Spanish trawler
fleet

Fishing dispute

'I'm doing the Spanish marathon – it's a lot shorter'

Fishing dispute

'He used to be a fisherman'

'What a cheek! The Spanish
are fishing in the High Street'

The Budget

'I've worked out it would be
more prudent to get drunk
than to drive home'

'I've turned off the heating –
I'm saving up for a packet
of cigarettes'

The recession

High noon on the high street and even the
utilities feel the pinch

The recession

'I bought these on Saturday but I now realise I was coming out of recession too fast'

'First I'm given a pay cut and now my thumb's on fire'

The recession

'My card keeps coming
out in sympathy'

'I suppose I should have
seen this coming'

The recession

Fat cats

'We've come to read the chief executive's pay slip'

'It's discreetly saying that your salary is distasteful'

Fat cats

'We've just paid the
chairman so I'm afraid
we're right out of money'

'What a terrible nightmare!
I dreamt you were paid
what you're worth'

Barings goes bust

'Miss Robins, jump out
of the window for
me, please'

'I don't know how to tell you
this, Mr Leeson, but we've
lost your luggage'

Barings goes bust

Health of the nation

Prescription charges go up … again

Health of the nation

'The lawyers will be doing
their rounds shortly'

'Pointy little knife thingy...
those sort of sugar tongs...'

Theatre sister charged for
operating on patient

Health of the nation

'Ahhh, how sweet, a teeny weeny little pay award'

'I'm just going to take my blood pressure'

Nurses pay award is the usual paltry sum

Health of the nation

'That'll be handy for Londoners who want to get to a hospital'

'Sorry to call you out, doctor, but it never seems to happen during surgery hours'

Famous London hospitals to close as doctors complain about increasing night visits

Law and order

'I'm arresting you for impersonating a member of the Citizens' Patrol'

As the police launch a new offensive on street crime the neighbourhood watch scheme ups the ante…

Law and order

'By the way – I'm holding
Mr Jones in our broom
cupboard for questioning'

'I remember when you could
leave your front door open and
expect something to be stolen'

Crime figures down

Crime and punishment

Juvenile criminals sent on adventure holidays
in rehabilitation attempt causes a public outcry

Crime and punishment

Dear Mum,
We've got enough guns; next time just send the cake.

'For goodness sake don't light the candles'

Privately run Whitemoor prison suffers escape attempts and explosives finds

Crime and punishment

'How long do you intend to stay, sir?'

Prisoners escape Parkhurst on the I.O.W and duplicate key found within a couple of miles from the jail

Crime and punishment

'Being in Parkhurst is no excuse for not visiting your mother'

'No, my husband's in prison – he could walk in here at any moment'

ID by any other name

'I regard ID cards as an
infringement of
my liberties'

'I'm going to pay someone
better looking to pose for
my driving licence photo'

Plans announced to add photographs to driving
licences

The modern military

'I'm going to make civilians out of you lot'

'My interior decorator has taken it very badly'

Cuts announced in all branches of the Services as huge decorating bills revealed for high ranking officer accommodations

The modern military

'On second thoughts, just shake my hand, Hardy'

GAYS IN THE ARMY?

'Who goes there — just a good friend, or foe?'

Army says no thanks to homosexuals

The modern military

'Now it's getting nasty –
Saddam is producing
his own brand of cola'

Saddam's last stand

The modern military

'And I got that one for not getting pregnant'

'I'm part of a Rapid Bewilderment Force - I fail to understand events as soon as they've happened'

Arms to Iraq

'Who sold them that?'

'Specialist subject — what Jonathan Aitken didn't know between 1988-1990'

The scandal continues with Aitken in Paris and the incredible hotel bill

Motorway madness

'He's not stuck, he's protesting against the M65'

'We've got a problem – a veal calf farm is being closed down to make way for a motorway'

New Age tribesmen stage live-in protests against road expansion

Live exports

'I don't mind going abroad
but not on the same ferry
as the England fans'

'One . . . two . . . three . . .'

Mass public protests against the live export of
animals for the continental butchery trade

Live exports

'I think it's a trick'

'Don't order the Veal Surprise'

Europe

'We've got this down as
a 30 acre olive grove'

E.C. bureaucracy encourages large scale fraud

Europe

'Well, we didn't win the
lottery — let's try for
a £2m EC subsidy next week'

Euro-non-star-ter

'£95 ! I could fly for less than that,' said Thomas

'Tell them they're going through the tunnel'

Weather

*'Either the tunnel is leaking
or we've arrived in Europe'*

*'I just heard a
cuckoo sneeze'*

Europe floods as England freezes

Sporting glory

The season of match-fixing begins

Sporting glory

'It's football practice
tomorrow so bring a
briefcase full of cash'

Sporting glory

'I had that Dennis Wise in the back of my cab'

Professional footballer charged with assault

Sporting glory

Cricket lovely cricket ... England down under, in more ways than one

Sporting glory

'It's good to see an England player catch something for a change'

Sporting glory

Ooh, aah, Cantona ... home and away, as the
Man Utd star is sent down for assaulting a
Crystal Palace fan

Sporting glory

'I suppose boxing keeps the
elderly off the streets'

'And remember, no punching
below the cardigan'

The ageing George Foreman makes a heavy-
weight comeback

Religion in the nineties

'If anyone here knows of any reason why these two people cannot move their stuff into a flat...'

'Can a bishop go either way?'

The C. of E. hits the headlines condoning living in sin, and with a gay bishop

That family ...

The Queen strikes oil at Windsor as her family
keep booksellers beaming

That family ...

'If we stay married for much
longer people will think
we're lower class'

'I take it the King decided
against a mediated divorce
settlement then?'

Charles and Diana admit they are considering
legal separation

The National Lottery

And the rest ...

'Which herbs and plants do your people use to preserve share prices?'

'I put cucumber slices on my eyes to stop me reading any upsetting reports'

How green is your Bodyshop ... share price tumbles as USA questions their ethics

And the rest ...

'We have travelled many millions of miles using our fathers' credit cards'

Runaway makes it to Malaysia

And the rest...

'Wow, this ribbon was made right here in Britain'

QE2 refit a disaster as new shipbuilding contract goes to foreign company

And the rest ...

'We're clamping down on excessive points'

More sporting fiascos

And the rest ...

'I can still remember when most British cars were Japanese'

Another British institution bites the dust

Holes in the road cause airport chaos

And the rest ...

'I had that nightmare again,
the one where Ffyona Campbell
takes me for a walk'

'I wonder how they chose
those numbers'

Round the world achievement
for British girl

And the rest ...

'Local or general anaesthetic?'

'Lookout, it's cheese!'

Man operated on in-flight as government announces new nutritional guidelines

And the rest…

'Grimby, you're £350,000 late'

BT announce they make £111 per second … as others struggle to survive

And the rest ...

'I changed my mind about
where to put it'

'I couldn't track down
the rest of the staff'

Shell bow to protests over the
jettisoning of Brent Spar

And the CSA gives way to
public pressure

And the rest...

The annual Turner commotion and the annual showgirl meets politician in the battle for the front page

And the rest ...

'It's time you thought
about your pension, son'

'This could be a big
earner, Mr Dumpty'

Bigger pensions for smokers

And the rest ...

'Let's play doctors and nurses – I'll report you for incompetence'

Shop-a-doctor

Ballroom dancing to become Olympic sport

And the rest ...

Report says private security
firms are employing crooks